FOOD SECURITY IN PRACTICE

Social Accounting Matrices and Multiplier Analysis

An Introduction with Exercises

Clemens Breisinger, Marcelle Thomas, and James Thurlow

About IFPRI

The International Food Policy Research Institute (IFPRI®) was established in 1975 to identify and analyze alternative national and international strategies and policies for meeting food needs of the developing world on a sustainable basis, with particular emphasis on low-income countries and on the poorer groups in those countries. While the research effort is geared to the precise objective of contributing to the reduction of hunger and malnutrition, the factors involved are many and wide-ranging, requiring analysis of underlying processes and extending beyond a narrowly defined food sector. The Institute's research program reflects worldwide collaboration with governments and private and public institutions interested in increasing food production and improving the equity of its distribution. Research results are disseminated to policymakers, opinion formers, administrators, policy analysts, researchers, and others concerned with national and international food and agricultural policy.

About IFPRI Food Security in Practice series

The Food Security in Practice technical guide series is designed for development practitioners. The guides are based on IFPRI research and enable project personnel in the field to take research from analysis to action. Each volume addresses informational and methodological issues that practitioners confront during the life of a project and presents the lessons learned from research on specific development issues. Relevant research and operational concepts are explained in easy-to-understand ways. Additional information pertaining to research analyses, methodologies, and results is available from IFPRI.

FOOD SECURITY IN PRACTICE

Social Accounting Matrices and Multiplier Analysis

An Introduction with Exercises

Clemens Breisinger, Marcelle Thomas, and James Thurlow

Updated April 2010

International Food Policy Research Institute
2033 K Street, N.W.
Washington, D.C. 20006-1002
U.S.A.
Telephone +1-202-862-5600
www.ifpri.org

How to cite this book: Breisinger, C., M. Thomas, and J. Thurlow. 2009. Social accounting matrices and multiplier analysis: An introduction with exercises. Food Security in Practice technical guide 5. Washington, D.C.: International Food Policy Research Institute.

DOI: 10.2499/9780896297838fsp5

Library of Congress Cataloging-in-Publication Data

Breisinger, Clemens.
Social accounting matrices and multiplier analysis : an introduction with exercises / Clemens Breisinger, Marcelle Thomas, and James Thurlow.
p. cm. — (Food security in practice ; no. 5)
Includes bibliographical references.
ISBN 978-0-89629-783-8 (alk. paper)
1. Social accounting--Mathematical models. 2. Microsoft Excel (Computer file) I. Thomas, Marcelle. II. Thurlow, James. III. Title.
HC79.I5B72 2009
330.0285'554—dc22

2009044463

Contents

Acknowledgments

This introductory guide to social accounting matrices and multiplier analysis was originally prepared for a series of workshops held in Ghana. We are grateful to the course participants for helping us refine the materials. In particular we thank Prof. Nsowah-Nuamah, Magnus Duncan, and Shashi Kolavalli for facilitating the workshops. Some of the teaching slides accompanying this guidebook were adapted from course materials produced and generously shared by Rob Davies and Dirk van Seventer. We also thank Suresh Babu, Xinshen Diao, Steve Haggblade, Sam Morley, and two anonymous reviewers for their comments and suggestions. Finally, we thank the United States Agency for International Development (USAID) and the German Agency for Technical Cooperation (GTZ) for funding the Ghana courses and the development of this guidebook.

Financial Contributors and Partners

IFPRI's research and capacity-strengthening and communications activities are made possible by its financial contributors and partners. IFPRI receives its principal funding from governments, private foundations, and international and regional organizations, most of which are members of the Consultative Group on International Agricultural Research (CGIAR). IFPRI gratefully acknowledges the generous unrestricted funding from Australia, Canada, China, Denmark, Finland, France, Germany, India, Ireland, Italy, Japan, the Netherlands, Norway, South Africa, Sweden, Switzerland, the United Kingdom, the United States, and the World Bank.

Introduction

This training guide introduces development practitioners, policy analysts, and students to social accounting matrices (SAMs) and their use in policy analysis. There are already a number of books that explain the System of National Accounts and SAM multipliers—some of these are recommended at the end of this training guide. However, most books tend to be quite technical and move quickly from an introduction to more complex applications. By contrast, this guidebook uses a series of hands-on exercises to gradually introduce SAMs and multiplier analysis. It therefore complements more theoretical SAM and multiplier literature and provides a first step for development practitioners and students wishing to understand the strengths and limitations of these economic tools. It is also useful for policy analysts and researchers embarking on more complex SAM-based methodologies. One such methodology is computable general equilibrium (CGE) modeling, for which IFPRI has also developed a series of introductory exercises and a standard modeling framework.[1]

The course is designed around five Microsoft Excel-based exercises. Each exercise begins with a background discussion, an outline of the task, and hints to help get you started. Each task and its solution can be downloaded from the IFPRI website (http://www.ifpri.org/publication/social-accounting-matrices-and-multiplier-analysis). After finishing each task, you can check your answers by looking at the completed worksheets in the "Solution" files. You should also return to the guidebook, where we often discuss the results. Although all exercises are based on the Ghanaian economy in 2007, the materials can be adapted to other countries and years.

The course materials are designed for trainers and for self-learning and will be useful for both newcomers to the topic as well as people who wish to refresh their knowledge of SAMs and multiplier analysis. The exercises gradually introduce the concepts and skills that you would need to conduct your own multiplier analysis:

Exercise 1 explains the basic structure of a SAM and outlines the data required to build this database. In Task 1 you will construct an aggregate "macro" SAM for Ghana using data from the national accounts, government budget, and balance of payments. At the end of this task, you should be familiar with the structure of a SAM and how to use various national economic data to assemble a macro-SAM.

Exercise 2 describes the various cells of a more disaggregated SAM. In Task 2, you will use the Ghana SAM to calculate key macro- and microeconomic indicators. At the end of this task, you should be able to interpret a SAM and understand the broad economic structure of an economy.

Exercise 3 introduces the concepts of "economic linkages" and "multiplier effects." In Task 3, you will use the coefficients in the Ghana SAM to calculate the round-by-round multiplier effects of increasing agricultural production. At the end of this task, you should be familiar with economic linkages and how they lead to indirect effects and multiplier processes.

Exercise 4 derives a mathematical formula for calculating multiplier effects. In Task 4, you will construct a simple or "unconstrained" multiplier model in Excel using the Ghana SAM. At the end of this task, you should know how to program the multiplier formula into Excel and interpret the results from a multiplier model.

Exercise 5 extends the simple multiplier model from the previous exercise by dropping the assumption that sectors are unconstrained in their ability to increase output when demand rises. In Task 5, you will interpret the results of a pre-programmed "constrained" multiplier model, where the output of some sectors is fixed (a "semi-input-output" model). At the end of this task, you should understand the importance of supply constraints and how to run and interpret simulations using this more complicated model.

The folder containing the exercises and their solutions also includes a Microsoft PowerPoint presentation covering some of the background materials used in the five exercises. In addition, the folder contains Handouts 1 and 2, which, like the two appendixes in this guide, summarize the derivation of the multiplier formulas used in Exercises 4 and 5.

[1] See Microcomputers in Policy Research Series 4 (www.ifpri.org/pubs/microcom/micro4.htm) and Series 5 (http://www.ifpri.org/pubs/microcom/micro5.htm).

Exercise 1: Composition of a SAM

What is a SAM?

One way of depicting the economy is the circular flow diagram shown in Figure 1, which captures all transfers and real transactions between sectors and institutions. Productive activities purchase land, labor, and capital inputs from the factor markets, and intermediate inputs from commodity markets, and use these to produce goods and services. These are supplemented by imports (M) and then sold through commodity markets to households (C), the government (G), investors (I), and foreigners (E). In the circular flow diagram, each institution's expenditure becomes another institution's income. For example, household and government purchases of commodities provide the incomes producers need to continue the production process. Additional inter-institutional transfers, such as taxes and savings, ensure that the circular flow of incomes is closed. In other words, all income and expenditure flows are accounted for, and there are no leakages from the system.

A SAM is also a representation of the economy. More specifically, it is an accounting framework that assigns numbers to the incomes and expenditures in the circular flow diagram. A SAM is laid out as a square matrix in which each row and column is called an "account." Table 1 shows the SAM that corresponds to the circular flow diagram in Figure 1. Each of the boxes in the diagram is an account in the SAM. Each cell in the matrix represents, by convention, a flow of funds from a column account to a row account. For example, the circular flow diagram shows private consumption spending as a flow of funds from households to commodity markets. In the SAM, it is entered in the household column and commodity row. The underlying principle of double-entry accounting requires that, for each account in the SAM, total revenue equals total expenditure. This means that an account's row and column totals must be equal.

Figure 1. Circular flow diagram of the economy

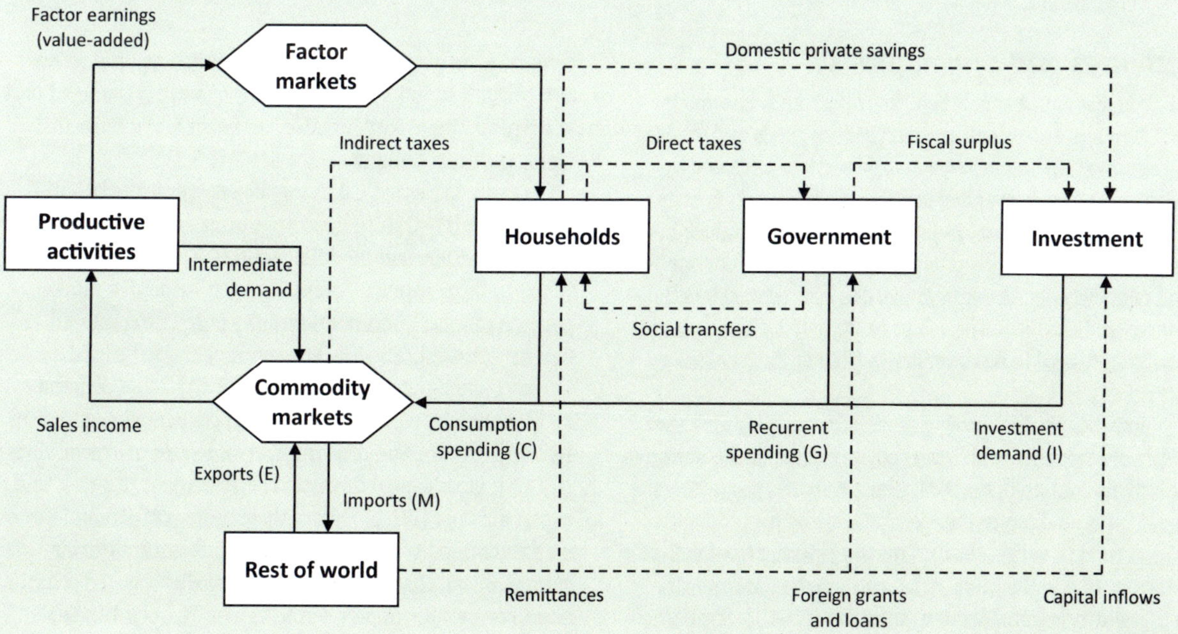

Table 1. Basic structure of a SAM

		Expenditure columns							
		Activities C1	**Commodities C2**	**Factors C3**	**Households C4**	**Government C5**	**Savings and investment C6**	**Rest of world C7**	**Total**
Income rows	**Activities R1**		Domestic supply						Activity income
	Commodities R2	Intermediate demand			Consumption spending (C)	Recurrent spending (G)	Investment demand (I)	Export earnings (E)	Total demand
	Factors R3	Value-added							Total factor income
	Households R4			Factor payments to households		Social transfers		Foreign remittances	Total household income
	Government R5		Sales taxes and import tariffs		Direct taxes			Foreign grants and loans	Government income
	Savings and investment R6				Private savings	Fiscal surplus		Current account balance	Total savings
	Rest of world R7		Import payments (M)						Foreign exchange outflow
	Total	Gross output	Total supply	Total factor spending	Total household spending	Government expenditure	Total investment spending	Foreign exchange inflow	

Activities and commodities

The SAM distinguishes between "activities" and "commodities." Activities are the entities that produce goods and services, and commodities are those goods and services produced by activities. They are separated because sometimes an activity produces more than one kind of commodity (by-products). Similarly, commodities can be produced by more than one kind of activity: for example, maize can be produced by small- or large-scale farmers. The values in the activity accounts are usually measured in producer prices (that is, farm or factory gate prices).

Activities produce goods and services by combining the factors of production with intermediate inputs. This is shown in the activity column of the SAM, where activities pay factors the wages, rents, and profits they generate during the production process (that is, value-added). This is a payment from activities to factors, and so the value-added entry in the SAM appears in the activity column and the factor row [R3-C1]. Similarly, intermediate demand is a payment from activities to commodities [R2-C1]. Adding together value-added and intermediate demand gives gross output. The information on production technologies contained in the activity column is the input part of a typical "input–output table," or factor and intermediate inputs per unit of output.

Commodities are either supplied domestically [R1-C2] or imported [R7-C2]. Indirect sales taxes and import tariffs are paid on these commodities [R5-C2]. This means that the values in the commodity accounts are measured at market prices. A number of economic entities purchase commodities. As discussed, activities buy commodities to be used as intermediate inputs for production [R2-C1]. Final demand for commodities consists of household consumption spending [R2-C4], government consumption, or recurrent expenditure [R2-C5], gross capital formation or investment [R2-C6], and export demand [R2-C7]. All of these sources of demand make up the commodity row (payments by different entities for commodities). On their own, the commodity row and column accounts are sometimes referred to as a "Supply–Use Table," or the total supply of commodities and their different kinds of uses or demands.

The SAM in Table 1 shows only single activity and commodity rows and columns. However, a SAM generally contains a number of different activities and commodities. For example, activities may be divided into agriculture, industry, and services. The information needed to construct these detailed activity and commodity accounts is usually found in a country's national accounts, input–output table and/or supply–use table.[2] All of these data are usually published by a country's statistical bureau.

Domestic institutions

A SAM is different from an input–output matrix because it not only traces the income and expenditure flows of activities and commodities, but it also contains complete information on different institutional accounts, such as households and the government. Households are usually the ultimate owners of the factors of production, and so they receive the incomes earned by factors during the production process [R4-C3].[3] They also receive transfer payments from the government [R4-C5] (for example, social security and pensions) and from the rest of the world [R4-C7] (such as remittances received from family members working abroad). Households then pay taxes directly to the government [R5-C4] and purchase commodities [R2-C4]. The remaining income is then saved (or dis-saved if expenditures exceed incomes) [R6-C4].[4] Information in household accounts is usually drawn from national accounts and household surveys from the country's statistics bureau.

The government receives transfer payments from the rest of the world [R5-C7] (such as foreign grants and development assistance). This is added to all of the different tax incomes to determine total government revenues. The government uses these revenues to pay for recurrent consumption spending [R2-C5] and transfers to households [R4-C5]. The difference between total revenues and expenditures is the fiscal surplus (or deficit, if expenditures exceed revenues) [R6-C5]. Information on the government accounts is normally drawn from public-sector budgets published by a country's ministry of finance.

Savings, investment, and the foreign account

According to the ex post accounting identity, investment or gross capital formation, which includes changes in stocks or inventories, must equal total savings. So far we have accounted for private savings [R6-C4] and public savings [R6-C5]. The difference between total domestic savings and total investment demand is total capital inflows from abroad, or what is called the current account balance [R6-C7]. This is also equal to the difference between foreign exchange receipts (exports and foreign transfers received) and expenditures (imports and government transfers to foreigners). Information on the current account (or rest of world) is drawn from the balance of payments, which is usually published by a country's central bank.

Balancing a SAM

The information needed to build a SAM comes from a variety of sources, such as national accounts, household surveys, government budgets, and the balance of payments. Placing these data within the SAM framework almost always reveals inconsistencies between the incomes and expenditures of each account. For example, government spending in national accounts may not be the same as what is reported in the government budget. A number of statistical estimation techniques exist to balance SAM accounts or reconcile incomes and expenditures. Cross-entropy estimation is generally the preferred method. More information on this approach can be found in various IFPRI discussion papers.[5]

TASK 1
CONSTRUCTING A MACRO-SAM FOR GHANA

In Task 1, you will build an aggregate macro-SAM using data from Ghana for the year 2007. You should construct the Ghana SAM on the worksheet "Task 1: Construct the Ghana macro-SAM" in the Excel file "Task 1 Worksheet.xls." The four datasets that you will need to complete the SAM are on the following worksheets:

- National accounts (GDP at factor cost)
- National accounts (GDP at market prices)
- Government budget
- Balance of payments

The datasets have already been balanced so there are no inconsistencies between incomes and expenditures. Using the SAM structure shown in Table 1, enter the data from the four datasets into the cells of the macro-SAM in order to produce a balanced 2007 SAM for Ghana.

Hints and tips

1. The Ghana macro-SAM is slightly more disaggregated than the one shown in Table 1—it splits the factor account into labor and capital.
2. It is usually easiest if you enter the accounts from left to right. In other words, you should first balance the activity account, and then move onto the commodity account. Proceed across the accounts until you reach the final "rest of the world" account.

3. Do not just type the actual numbers from the datasets into the macro-SAM. Rather, it is better practice to link the macro-SAM entries to the respective datasets. You do this by typing "=" followed by the cell reference where the data are stored. Linking the macro-SAM to the four datasets will allow you to trace back the source of each cell entry.

4. The row and column totals are automatically calculated for you as you fill in the cells. The macro-SAM worksheet also calculates the difference between row and column totals, which should help you identify missing entries as you construct the SAM.

5. The four datasets contain all of the information you need to complete the macro-SAM. However, not all data provided in the datasets are relevant. Below are some tips on the kinds of data you will find on each worksheet and how to calculate some of the more complicated cell entries in the macro-SAM.

   National accounts (GDP at factor cost)

   a. You will need to use the capital–labor value-added shares to split GDP at factor cost into its labor and capital components.

   b. To calculate intermediate demand, you will need to use the intermediate input to value-added ratio.

   c. Household factor income is the total return to labor and capital.

   d. Producer taxes, which are one type of indirect taxes, are on this worksheet.

   National accounts (GDP at market prices)

   e. This worksheet contains information on household consumption spending, government recurrent spending, and investment demand. It also has total export earnings and import payments.

   f. The difference between GDP at factor cost and GDP at market prices is that the latter includes sales taxes and import tariffs (indirect taxes).

   Government budget

   g. Indirect taxes on this worksheet include sales and import and export taxes.

   h. Direct taxes include personal and corporate taxes. In our aggregate SAM, we combine these two taxes together and charge them both to households.

   Balance of payments

   i. Ghana ran a current account deficit in 2007. You should therefore enter a negative number into the macro-SAM (foreign dis-savings).

   j. Exports and imports consist of traded goods and services. The balance of payments often nets out exported and imported services, so you will have to use the value of total imports and exports from national accounts.

6. Information on household savings is missing from the datasets. However, we know that incomes must equal expenditures in a balanced SAM, so household savings can be calculated as a residual once we have entered all of the other cells.

Discussion of Task 1

Once you have completed Task 1, you can check your answers by opening the file "Task 1 Solution.xls." The numbers contained in the solution's macro-SAM are color-coded to make it easier to locate the relevant information. Also, all entries are linked to their sources so that you can check the origin and mode of calculation of all macro-SAM cells. By completing this first exercise you will have learned how to construct a balanced and consistent macro-SAM. In the next exercise, we will construct a more disaggregated SAM for Ghana and then discuss the meanings of each cell entry in greater detail.

NOTES

2. For a description of the System of National Accounts, see http://unstats.un.org/unsd/sna1993/introduction.asp

3. In our SAM and exercises, we will exclude corporate enterprises. For simplicity, we assume that profits (or gross operating surplus) are paid directly to households (i.e., households' direct taxes include corporate taxes).

4. If total household expenditures exceed incomes, then a negative value would appear in the savings cell entry.

5. See the IFPRI discussion papers TMD-33 (www.ifpri.org/divs/TMD/DP/tmdp33.htm), also published as Robinson et al. 2001; TMD-58 (www.ifpri.org/divs/tmd/dp/tmdp58.htm); and TMD-64 (www.ifpri.org/divs/tmd/dp/tmdp64.htm).

Exercise 2: Analysis of a SAM

DETAILED DISCUSSION OF THE MACRO-SAM

In the previous exercise, you constructed an aggregate macro-SAM using 2007 data from Ghana. The balanced macro-SAM is shown in Table 2. In this background section we discuss each of the entries and identify where information can usually be found to construct a more disaggregated SAM. Cell entries are identified as row-column combinations and are valued in millions of Ghana cedi at 2007 prices.[6]

Value-added

[Labor, Activities: 9,717] and [Capital, Activities: 3,250]
Total value-added is the earnings received by the factors of production, such as the wages and salaries paid to labor and the profits paid to capital. Total value-added is also called "GDP at factor cost." Information on GDP for different sectors is usually found in national accounts. This was the case in Task 1, where Ghana's GDP at factor cost was reported for 14 sectors. Total value-added was split into labor and capital components using technology coefficients from Ghana's input–output table. The national capital–labor coefficient from Task 1 estimates that 75 percent of GDP is generated by labor, implying that Ghana is a "labor-intensive" economy.

Intermediate demand

[Commodities, Activities: 12,029]
Intermediate demand is the goods and services used in the production process. This was a single number in the macro-SAM in Task 1, and so it could only describe the national ratio of spending on factor to nonfactor inputs. However, a more detailed SAM that disaggregates activities and commodities would

Table 2. 2007 Ghana macro-SAM (millions of cedi)

		Activities C1	Commodities C2	Factors: Labor C3-1	Factors: Capital C3-2	Households C4	Government C5	Savings and investment C6	Rest of world C7	Total
Activities R1			24,996							24,996
Commodities R2		12,029				12,142	1,805	4,680	5,151	35,807
Factors	Labor R3-1	9,717								9,717
	Capital R3-2	3,250								3,250
Households R4				9,717	3,250		1,387		2,001	16,354
Government R5			2,372			940			739	4,052
Savings and investment R6						3,272	860		548	4,680
Rest of world R7			8,439							8,439
Total		24,996	35,807	9,717	3,250	16,354	4,052	4,680	8,439	

reveal differences in production technologies across sectors. For example, it would show which sectors use more fuel per value-unit of output. This information is useful when determining the effects of policies and external shocks on the economy. Information on sectors' production technologies is drawn from an input–output (IO) table. If an IO table does not exist, or if it does not include all sectors—as was the case in Ghana—then it is necessary to estimate production technologies using agricultural farm budgets and industrial surveys.

Factor income distribution

[Households, Labor: 9,717] and [Households, Capital: 3,250]

Factor incomes in the macro-SAM were paid to an aggregate household account. However, most SAMs split households into different groups, such as rural and urban. This information allows us to assess distributional impacts from policies. As a simple example, if our SAM shows that low-income households rely more on labor earnings than higher-income households, then policies that increase production in labor-intensive sectors should disproportionately benefit poorer households. Obviously, the greater the disaggregation, the more we can refine our assessment. Thus, the distribution of factor incomes is an important part of a SAM. This information is usually drawn from labor force or household income surveys. There may also be factors payments to nonhousehold accounts. For example, some of the profits earned by capital may be paid to foreign investors (for instance, mining rents) or to the government (such as state-owned enterprises). For simplicity we ignore these flows in our exercises.

Private consumption

[Commodities, Households: 12,142]

Households use most of their incomes to purchase commodities for consumption. Although the macro-SAM contains a single entry, most SAMs disaggregate private consumption across different commodities and household groups because households' consumption patterns vary, especially across income groups. For example, poorer households usually spend a larger share of their income on food than do wealthier households, and so changes in the supply of foods will affect poorer households more. These differences can influence the distributional impacts of policies and external shocks. Information on consumption patterns can be drawn from household income and expenditure surveys, such as the World Bank's Living Conditions Monitoring Surveys.

Government recurrent spending and investment demand

[Commodities, Government: 1,805] and [Commodities, Investment: 4,680]

Total absorption in an economy consists of private consumption, as well as public consumption spending and investment demand. Public consumption or recurrent expenditure consists of the goods and services purchased to maintain government function. Investment demand consists of both public and private gross capital formation, such as spending on roads, schools, and residential housing. Investment demand is therefore mainly for commodities like cement and construction services. This information is usually drawn from national accounts, government budgets, and supply-use tables.

Foreign trade

[Commodities, Rest of world: 8,439] and [Rest of world, Commodities: 5,151]

Information on export earnings and import payments comes from three sources. National accounts and the balance of payments provide aggregate estimates of international trade in goods and services. Most SAMs include further detail on specific commodities groups, the information for which is compiled from a country's customs or trade data.

Government taxes

[Government, Commodities: 2,374] and [Government, Households: 940]

The government generates revenue from direct and indirect taxes. Direct taxes include personal (pay as you earn) and corporate taxes imposed on domestic institutions, such as households and enterprises. Because we do not distinguish between households and enterprises, direct taxes appear as a single value in our Ghana macro-SAM. Similarly, we do not distinguish between the various indirect taxes imposed on commodities, such as sales and export taxes and import tariffs.[7] Information on tax rates on different commodities and households can usually be obtained from tax authorities, customs data, and household income and expenditure surveys.

Remittances and social transfers

[Households, Government: 1,387] and [Households, Rest of world: 2,001]

Apart from factor payments, households also receive transfers from the government and the rest of the world. Government transfers include social security payments and public pensions. Foreign receipts usually include remittances from family members living and working abroad. Conversely, households might also remit incomes to family members living abroad. In the macro-SAM, this could be reflected as a positive entry in the cell [Rest of world, Households] or, as in the Ghana SAM, as a negative addition to the cell [Households, Rest of world].

Grants, loans, and interest on foreign debt

[Government, Rest of world: 739]
Many governments in low-income countries receive grants and loans from development partners and foreign financial institutions to cover recurrent spending and capital investments. These are direct payments from the rest of the world to the government. Conversely, foreign debt requires interest payments, which are positive payments from the government to the rest of the world. Alternatively, interest payments can be treated as a negative receipt from the rest of the world. This is the convention adopted in the Ghana macro-SAM. Information on foreign grant transfers to and from the government is drawn from government budgets and the balance of payments.

Domestic and foreign savings

[Savings, Households: 3,272], [Savings, Government: 860], and [Savings, Rest of world: 548]
The difference between incomes and expenditures is savings (or dis-savings if expenditures exceed incomes). For the government account, this is equal to the fiscal surplus/deficit and for the rest of world account it is the current account balance. This information is documented in the government budget and balance of payments. However, information on domestic private savings is rarely recorded in developing datasets. Therefore, household savings is often treated as a residual when balancing a macro-SAM.

TASK 2
INTERPRETING THE GHANA MICRO-SAM

In Task 2, you will calculate various macroeconomic indicators using the information contained in a SAM and then answer a number of questions regarding Ghana's economic structure. The SAM can be found in the Excel file "Task 2 Worksheet.xls." The SAM is more detailed than the one constructed in Exercise 1. Activities are now disaggregated across seven sectors, and households are split into rural and urban groups. We will refer to this as the "Ghana micro-SAM." Using the SAM, you are asked to calculate and interpret production shares, commodity shares, demand shares, household income and expenditure shares, and macroeconomic indicators. The instructions and questions for Task 2 can be found on the Excel worksheet.

Hints and tips

1. It is good practice to link your calculations to the SAM entries. This will allow you to easily trace back the data used in your calculations.
2. Hints are included in the Excel file. For example, next to some tables there is a blue number, which is the correct answer that should appear in the table. Check this number with your own answer to make sure you are on the right track.

DISCUSSION OF TASK 2

GDP shares

By calculating the share of GDP generated by each sector, we are determining which sectors contributed the most to factors' income or value-added. Our findings show that Ghana depends heavily on agriculture, with the sector contributing 35.1 percent to GDP at factor cost. Utilities and construction also account for a large share of GDP (14.9 percent). The third largest sector (12.9 percent) is the government, which produces goods and services like housing, health, and education. The most labor-intensive sectors in the SAM are agriculture, trade, and public services. For example, 92.6 percent of agriculture value-added is paid to labor. By contrast, the most capital-intensive sector in Ghana is mining, where capital contributes 66.8 percent of total value-added. Together these calculations describe the key *structural characteristics* of production in the economy.

Gross output shares

By calculating the share of each factor and commodity payment in the value of gross output, we are determining sectors' *production technologies*. In other words, we are calculating the amount of each input required to produce a unit of each sector's output. We found that, in Ghana, manufactured goods are usually the most important intermediate input. In the mining sector, for example, manufactured inputs account for 29.3 percent of the value of output. This means that for each 100 cedis-worth of mining output, 29.3 cedi must be spent on manufactured inputs. Manufactured inputs are also important for the production of manufactured goods themselves (29.2 percent) and for trade and transport (39.3 percent). In turn, trade and transport is a key input into most sectors, especially manufacturing, agriculture, private services, and public services. This input payment captures the cost of moving goods from farms and factories to the markets where they are sold to households, investors, and other demanders. Therefore, not surprisingly, trade and transport accounts for a large share of the cost of agricultural production. As we will see in the next section, information on sectors' production technologies is an important part of the SAM, because it allows us to estimate interdependency (or linkages) between sectors.

Trade shares

These calculations shed light on the structure of imports and exports. Ghana, like many low-income countries in Africa, relies on primary exports, such as agriculture (39.1 percent) and mining (26 percent). It uses these export earnings to pay for imported goods. Our calculations show that the majority of imports are manufactured goods (88.2 percent), agricultural products (6.8 percent), and private services (such as tourism) (4.9 percent).

Another way of understanding the relative importance of trade for different commodities is to calculate import penetration ratios (IPR) and export intensities (EI). The IPR is the share of imports in the value of total demand, and EI is the share of exports in the value of gross output.

$$Import\ penetration\ ratio\ (IPR) = \frac{Imports}{Total\ demand}$$

$$Export\ intensity\ (EI) = \frac{Exports}{Gross\ output}$$

Our calculated IPRs reveal that Ghana's manufacturing sector faces the most import competition, with 54.1 percent of total demand supplied by foreigners. By contrast, even though Ghana imports agricultural goods, these account for only a small part of total agricultural demand (7.4 percent). The Ghanaian economy is therefore reliant on foreign manufactured goods, but is fairly self-sufficient in agriculture. Our calculated EIs show almost all mining output is sold abroad (95.1 percent). Thanks to cocoa farmers, Ghanaian agriculture is also an export-intensive sector, with 28.5 percent of agricultural output exported.

Total demand shares

These calculations consider all the various sources of commodity demand, including intermediate, private and public consumption, investment, and exports. Our calculations show that manufacturing and agricultural goods are the largest components of private consumption spending (43.7 percent and 34.8 percent, respectively), followed by private services (15.1 percent). Not surprisingly, most government spending is on the outputs of the government services sector. Finally, investment demand is mainly accounted for by manufactures (56.1 percent) and electricity and construction (43.9 percent).

Household income and expenditure shares

Our SAM separates rural from urban households, which allows us to consider differences in how these two household groups earn and spend their incomes. For example, rural households spend most of their income on agricultural (33.8 percent) and manufactured goods (33 percent). This high manufacturing share may be surprising because we know that poorer rural households usually spend most of their income on food. This is, in fact, still the case in Ghana because manufacturing includes the food-processing sector, which means that most of rural demand for manufactured goods is actually demand for processed foods (for example, milled grains and meats). Urban households, on the other hand, spend less of their incomes on foods, as seen by the lower expenditure shares on both agricultural (19.5 percent) and manufactured goods (32 percent).

Total household incomes in our SAM comprise factor incomes (such as labor wages and capital profits) and nonfactor incomes (such as government transfers and foreign remittances). In our earlier calculations, we saw that production in Ghana is mostly labor intensive. Not surprisingly then, both rural and urban households earn most of their income from labor (69.6 percent and 51.3 percent, respectively). Both household groups are relatively equally reliant on capital earnings and government transfers. Capital earnings reflect the profits generated by nonfarm enterprises, such as rural food processors and urban manufactures factories. Finally, urban households are the largest recipients of foreign remittances. These transfers may be from family members working abroad. They constitute 17.5 percent of urban incomes compared to only 5.6 percent for rural households.

Macroeconomic shares

These indicators are based on GDP at factor cost, the fiscal balance, the current account balance, the level of private savings, and total imports and exports. GDP at factor cost is total capital and labor value added and, in our SAM, is equal to 12,967 million cedi. GDP at market prices is the sum of all final demands:

$$GDP = C + I + G + E - M$$

where C is private consumption
I is investment
G is government consumption
E is exports, and
M is imports.
GDP at market prices in our SAM is 15,339 million cedi.

The recurrent fiscal balance is 860 million cedi or 5.6 percent of GDP at market prices. The fact that it is positive means that Ghana's government ran a recurrent fiscal surplus in 2007. By contrast, the current account balance, which is recorded in the SAM as negative foreign savings, is a deficit of –548 million cedi or –3.6 percent of GDP. Most of the current account deficit is due to Ghana's large trade deficit of –3,228 million cedi or 21.4 percent of GDP: its total imports of 8,439 million cedi exceed total exports of 5,151 million cedi. Finally, the share of imports and exports in GDP (the trade-to-GDP ratio) is 88.6 percent, indicating that Ghana is a relatively open economy.

In summary, the information in the SAM reveals a great deal about a country's economic structure. Our calculations show a number of key characteristics of Ghana's economy. For example, we now know that Ghana is an agriculture-based and labor-intensive economy that relies heavily on agricultural and mining exports to pay for imported manufactures. However, primary exports are insufficient to pay for all exports, and the country runs a large current account deficit as a result. Ghana's government is an important part of the economy, and its fiscal surplus accounts for a significant share of total investment. However, though investment is a large part of GDP, private consumption is most important. Here we found that rural households spend a large share of income on agricultural goods and derive more of their incomes from labor than do urban households. These structural characteristics of the Ghanaian economy are important for explaining economic linkages and multiplier effects.

NOTES

6. In 2007 Ghana removed four zeros from its currency. The macro-SAM is therefore measured in "new" Ghana cedi. A detailed description of a 2005 Ghana SAM (Breisinger et al. 2005) using "old" Ghana cedi can be downloaded from the websites of IFPRI and Ghana Statistical Services (http://www.ifpri.org/dataset/ghana).

7. Many SAMs assign separate accounts to each type of tax. Tax revenues are then paid to the government account.

Exercise 3: Economic Linkages and Multiplier Effects

WHAT ARE ECONOMIC LINKAGES AND MULTIPLIER EFFECTS?

When we talk of "exogenous demand-side shocks" to an economy, we are referring to changes in export demand, government spending, or investment demand. The impacts of these shocks have both *direct* and *indirect* effects. Direct effects are those pertaining to the sector that is directly affected by the shock. For example, an exogenous increase in demand for Ghanaian agricultural exports has a direct impact on the agricultural sector. However, it may also have indirect effects stemming from agriculture's *linkages* to other sectors and parts of the economy. These indirect linkages can, in turn, be separated into *production* and *consumption* linkages. When we add up all direct and indirect linkages, we arrive at a measure of the shock's *multiplier* effect, or how much a direct effect is amplified or multiplied by indirect linkage effects.

Production linkages are determined by sectors' production technologies, which are contained in the input-output part of SAM. They are differentiated into *backward* and *forward* linkages.

- Backward production linkages are the demand for additional inputs used by producers to supply additional goods or services. For example, when agricultural production expands, it demands intermediate goods like fertilizers, machinery, and transport services. This demand then stimulates production in other sectors to supply these intermediate goods. The more input-intensive a sector's production technology is, the stronger its backward linkages are.
- Forward production linkages account for the increased supply of inputs to upstream industries. For example, when agricultural production expands, it can supply more goods to the food-processing sector, which stimulates manufacturing production. So the more important a sector is for upstream industries, the stronger its forward linkages will be.

Stronger forward and backward production linkages lead to larger multipliers. Traditional input-output multipliers measure the effects of production linkages only. They do not consider consumption linkages, which arise when an expansion of production generates additional incomes for factors and households, which are then used to purchase goods and services. For example, when agricultural production expands, it raises farmers' incomes, which are used to buy consumer goods. Depending on the share of tradable and nontradable goods in households' consumption baskets, domestic producers benefit from greater demand for their

Figure 2. Direct and indirect linkages

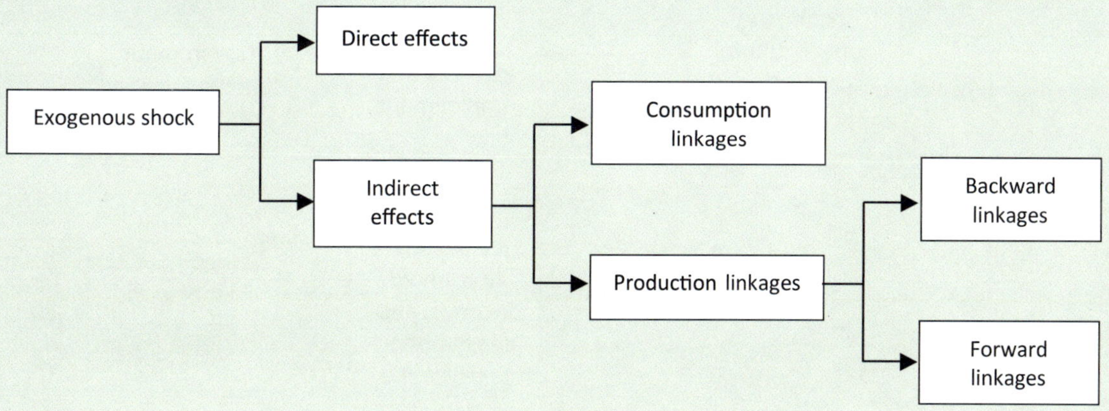

products. The size of consumption linkages depends on various factors, including the share of factor income distributed to households; the composition of the consumption basket; and the share of domestically supplied goods in consumer demand. Evidence from developing countries suggests that consumption linkage effects are much larger than production linkage effects: they account for 75–90 percent of total multiplier effects in sub-Saharan Africa and 50–60 percent in Asia (Haggblade, Hammer, and Hazell 1991). SAM multipliers therefore tend to be larger than input-output multipliers because they capture both production and consumption/income linkages.

Economic linkages are fairly static and are determined by the structural characteristics of an economy (that is, sectors' production technologies and the composition of households' consumption baskets). Multiplier effects, on the other hand, capture the combined effects of economic linkages over a period of time. For example, forward production linkages tell us that increasing agricultural production will stimulate production of processed foods by increasing the supply of inputs to this sector. This is the first-round linkage effect between agriculture and food processing. However, in the second round, the increase in processed food production will have additional forward production linkage effects to other sectors, such as to the restaurant sector, which uses processed foods as an intermediate input. Similarly, in the third round, the expansion of the restaurant sector will generate even more demand for other sectors. This process continues over many rounds as the effects of increasing agricultural production ripple throughout the economy, eventually becoming small enough that they effectively cease.

SAM multipliers measure the value of all production and consumption linkage effects. They capture direct and indirect effects in the first and all subsequent rounds of the circular income flow. More specifically, multipliers translate initial

Figure 3. Circular flow of income in the multiplier process

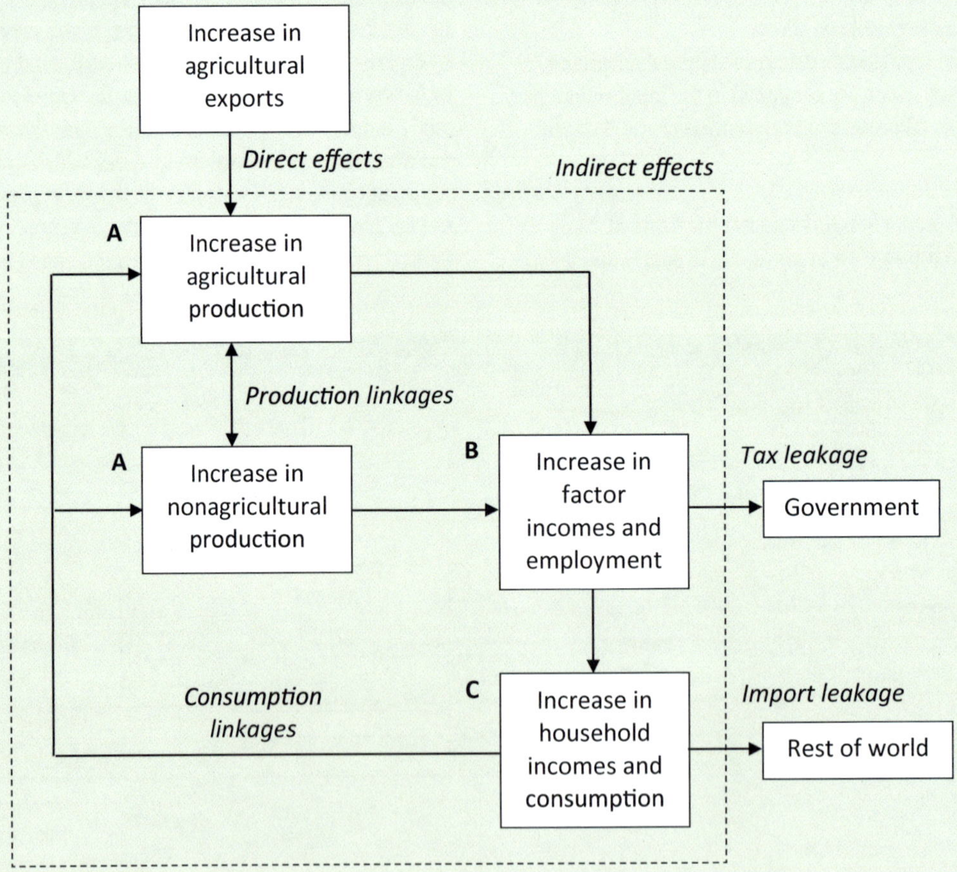

changes in exogenous demand (for example, increased agricultural export demand) into total production and income changes of endogenous accounts. Figure 3 illustrates this process.

Three types of multipliers can be distinguished from the figure. First, an *output multiplier* combines all direct and indirect (consumption and production) effects across multiple rounds and reports the final increase in gross output of all production activities. In Figure 3, this is the combined increase in agricultural and nonagricultural production (the two boxes marked "A"). Second, a *GDP multiplier* measures the total change value-added or factor incomes caused by direct and indirect effects (the box marked "B"). Finally, the *income multiplier* measures the total change in household incomes (the box marked "C").

The size of a multiplier depends on the structural characteristics of an economy. For example, a key determinant is the share of imported goods and services in households' consumption demand. If households consume domestically produced goods, then increasing household incomes will benefit domestic producers and the circular flow of income will lead to further rounds of indirect linkage effects. However, if households demand imported goods, then it is foreign producers who benefit and the indirect linkage effects will be smaller. Import demand is therefore a *leakage* from the circular flow of income. Similarly, when the government taxes factor incomes, it limits how much of the returns to production are earned to households, and so reduces consumption linkages. Ultimately, these kinds of leakages make the round-by-round effects slow down more quickly and reduce the total multiplier effect.

Task 3: Calculating Round-by-Round Linkage Effects

In Task 3, you will calculate backward production linkage effects during each round of the circular flow of income. In this task, you will use an aggregated two-sector version of the Ghana SAM to calculate input coefficients for the agricultural and nonagricultural sectors. Using these technical coefficients, you will then determine how downstream sectors benefit when agricultural production increases as a result of its use of intermediate inputs. The Ghana SAM and the flow chart (where you can complete this task) can be found in the file "Task 3 Worksheet.xls." Once you have completed the task, you can check your answer by looking at the file "Task 3 Solution.xls."

1. You are only asked to calculate backward production linkage effects. In Task 3 we ignore forward production and consumption linkages. We'll come back to these in later tasks.
2. Calculate input coefficients as in Task 2. It is good practice to link your calculations to the SAM entries because this allows you to trace back the data used in your calculations.
3. The first-round effect can be calculated by multiplying the direct increase in agricultural production (10) by the respective input coefficients for each of the two sectors to derive the additional increase in production in the second round.
4. To calculate second-round effects, repeat the process in hint 2, but this time start with the production increase from the end of round 1.
5. The numbers in blue are the correct answers for the neighboring cell entry.

Discussion of Task 3

This task demonstrates how sectors' production technologies (input coefficients) determine the size of multiplier effects. For example, increasing agricultural production has a larger linkage effect on nonagricultural production because the input coefficient on nonagricultural inputs (0.27) is much larger than the agricultural input coefficient (0.09). So at the end of the first round, the direct increase in agricultural production by 10 billion cedi leads to an indirect 2.71 billion-cedi increase in nonagricultural production, but only a 0.86 billion-cedi increase in agricultural production.

This task also shows how indirect effects become smaller from round to round. For example, the direct impact of increased agricultural export demand was a 10 billion-cedi increase in agricultural production. In the first round, total agricultural and nonagricultural production increased by 3.56 billion cedi (0.86 for agriculture and 2.71 for nonagriculture). In the second round the total increase was 1.74 billion cedi, and in the third round it was 0.89 billion cedi. If we were to continue calculating these linkage effects into subsequent rounds, we would see their values declining until they are virtually zero. At this point we can say that the multiplier process resulting from the increase in agricultural export demand has effectively ceased.

The importance of technical coefficients and the fact that linkages diminish after each round are important features of the multiplier process. They still apply even when forward production and consumption linkages are included in the calculation of multiplier effects. Task 3 has therefore explained the core concepts of the multiplier process and lays the foundation for calculating multipliers using matrix algebra, which is the objective of the next two exercises.

CA 600
ALCON

Exercise 4: Unconstrained SAM Multiplier Analysis

DERIVING THE UNCONSTRAINED MULTIPLIER FORMULA

In the previous task, we saw how labor-intensive it is to calculate round-by-round multiplier effects. Moreover, we excluded in our calculations the effects of forward production and consumption linkages. In this section we use matrix algebra to develop a formula for calculating total multiplier effects that will include all types of linkages and for all rounds. This formula will make it much easier to estimate multipliers. It will also allow us to consider not just output multipliers but also GDP and income multipliers, which can reveal important distributional effects from external demand-side shocks. In other words, we will calculate SAM multipliers rather than just input-output multipliers.

SAM multipliers are an extension of the classic Leontief input-output model. While the Leontief model concentrates on inter-industry production linkages, SAM-based models also include consumption linkages. Consumption linkages are included by making institutions like households and the government "endogenous."[8] The SAM multiplier approach therefore makes use of information on household factor endowments and income distribution. SAM multiplier models have been used for a wide range of issues from trade policies and macroeconomic shocks to farm-nonfarm linkages (see Pyatt and Round 1985; Haggblade and Hazell 1989; Reinert and Roland-Holst 1997; Bautista 2001; Diao et al. 2007).

The SAM multiplier framework can be used to estimate the impacts of changes in any of the exogenous demand accounts in the model. Because we are treating households as endogenous in the model, this leaves three possible sources of demand stimulus: export demand, government spending, and investment demand. Exogenous changes in demand for these accounts are then transmitted to endogenous accounts, including producing sectors and households.

Unconstrained multiplier models and their assumptions

Unconstrained multiplier models are the simplest kinds of multiplier models because they make a number of limiting assumptions. They assume that prices are fixed and that any changes in demand will lead to changes in physical output rather than prices. This in turn requires an additional assumption that the economy's factor resources are unlimited or unconstrained, so that any increase in demand can be matched by an increase in supply. Finally, the multiplier model assumes that all structural relationships between sectors and households in the economy are unaffected by exogenous changes in demand. In other words, the input coefficients of producers and the consumption patterns of households remain unchanged (that is, linkage effects are linear and there is no behavioral change).

In the next exercise, we will drop the assumption that supply in all sectors is unconstrained. Despite this extension to the model, the above assumptions remain serious limitations to SAM multiplier analysis. In some cases, these limitations provide sufficient justification to use more complex SAM-based methods, such as CGE models, which drop the assumption of fixed prices and unconstrained factor resources. However, SAM multipliers are an important step toward understanding these more complicated methods.

Unconstrained multiplier formula

We use matrix algebra to derive the unconstrained multiplier formula. We will use a two-sector SAM to illustrate the underlying equations, although the final multiplier formula can be applied to SAMs with any number of sectors. In Table 3, we replace the numbers in the SAM with letters or symbols so that we can refer to these in our equations. For example, X_1 refers to the value of gross output from activity 1, and Y refers to total household income.

Table 3. SAM entries expressed as letters or symbols

	Activities		Commodities		Factors	Households	Exogenous demand	Total
	A1	A2	C1	C2	F	H	E	
A1			X_1					X_1
A2				X_2				X_2
C1	Z_{11}	Z_{12}				C_1	E_1	Z_1
C2	Z_{21}	Z_{22}				C_2	E_2	Z_2
F	V_1	V_2						V
H					$V_1 + V_2$			Y
E			L_1	L_2		S		E
Total	X_1	X_2	Z_1	Z_2	V	Y	E	

where X is gross output of each activity (i.e., X_1 and X_2)
Z is total demand for each commodity (i.e., Z_1 and Z_2)
V is total factor income (equal to household income)
Y is total household income (equal to total factor income)
E is exogenous components of demand (government, investment, and exports)

We then divide each column in Table 3 by its column total to derive a coefficients matrix called "M-matrix." This is shown in Table 4. Note that the M-matrix excludes the exogenous components of demand.

Table 4. M-matrix

	Activities		Commodities		Factors	Households	Exogenous demand	Total
	A1	A2	C1	C2	F	H	E	
A1			$b_1=X_1/Z_1$					X_1
A2				$b_2=X_2/Z_2$				X_2
C1	$a_{11}=Z_{11}/X_1$	$a_{12}=Z_{12}/X_2$				$c_1=C_1/Y$	E_1	Z_1
C2	$a_{21}=Z_{21}/X_1$	$a_{22}=Z_{22}/X_2$				$c_2=C_2/Y$	E_2	Z_2
F	$v_1=V_1/X_1$	$v_2=V_2/X_2$						V
H					1			Y
E			$l_1=L_1/Z_1$	$l_2=L_2/Z_2$		$s=S/Y$		E
Total	1	1	1	1	1	1	E	

where a is technical coefficients (i.e., input or intermediate shares in production)
b is the share of domestic output in total demand
v is the share of value-added or factor income in gross output
l is the share of the value of total demand from imports or commodity taxes
c is household consumption expenditure shares
s is the household savings rate (i.e., savings as a share of total household income)

Using the symbols in the SAM, total demand Z in each sector is the sum of intermediate input demand, household consumption demand, and other exogenous sources of demand E, such as public consumption and investment. This is shown in Equations 4.1.

$$\begin{aligned} Z_1 &= a_{11}X_1 + a_{12}X_2 + c_1Y + E_1 \\ Z_2 &= a_{21}X_1 + a_{22}X_2 + c_2Y + E_2 \end{aligned} \tag{4.1}$$

From the SAM we know that gross output X is only part of total demand Z, as shown in Equations 4.2.

$$\begin{aligned} X_1 &= b_1Z_1 \\ X_2 &= b_2Z_2 \end{aligned} \tag{4.2}$$

We also know that total household income depends on the share of factors' earnings in each sector, as shown in Equation 4.3.

$$Y = v_1X_1 + v_2X_2 \tag{4.3}$$

Substituting Equation 4.2 into 4.3 gives the following identity for total income Y.

$$Y = v_1b_1Z_1 + v_2b_2Z_2 \tag{4.4}$$

We can now replace X and Y in Equations 4.1 using Equations 4.2 and 4.4.

$$\begin{aligned} Z_1 &= a_{11}b_1Z_1 + a_{12}b_2Z_2 + c_1(v_1b_1Z_1 + v_2b_2Z_2) + E_1 \\ Z_2 &= a_{21}b_1Z_1 + a_{22}b_2Z_2 + c_2(v_1b_1Z_1 + v_2b_2Z_2) + E_2 \end{aligned} \tag{4.5}$$

We move all terms, except for exogenous demand E, onto the left-hand side.

$$\begin{aligned} Z_1 - a_{11}b_1Z_1 - c_1v_1b_1Z_1 - a_{12}b_2Z_2 - c_1v_2b_2Z_2 &= E_1 \\ -a_{21}b_1Z_1 - c_2v_1b_1Z_1 + Z_2 - a_{22}b_2Z_2 - c_2v_2b_2Z_2 &= E_2 \end{aligned} \tag{4.6}$$

Finally, we group Z terms together.

$$\begin{aligned} (1 - a_{11}b_1 - c_1v_1b_1)Z_1 + (-a_{12}b_2 - c_1v_2b_2)Z_2 &= E_1 \\ (-a_{21}b_1 - c_2v_1b_1)Z_1 + (1 - a_{22}b_2 - c_2v_2b_2)Z_2 &= E_2 \end{aligned} \tag{4.7}$$

We can now use matrix algebra to convert Equations 4.7 into matrix format.

$$\begin{pmatrix} 1 - a_{11}b_1 - c_1v_1b_1 & -a_{12}b_2 - c_1v_2b_2 \\ -a_{21}b_1 - c_2v_1b_1 & 1 - a_{22}b_2 - c_2v_2b_2 \end{pmatrix} \begin{pmatrix} Z_1 \\ Z_2 \end{pmatrix} = \begin{pmatrix} E_1 \\ E_2 \end{pmatrix} \tag{4.8}$$

The first term in Equation 4.8 is the identity matrix (I) minus the coefficient matrix (M).

$$\begin{pmatrix} 1 - a_{11}b_1 - c_1v_1b_1 & -a_{12}b_2 - c_1v_2b_2 \\ -a_{21}b_1 - c_2v_1b_1 & 1 - a_{22}b_2 - c_2v_2b_2 \end{pmatrix} = I - M \tag{4.9}$$

If we rename the other two vectors Z and E we can express Equation 4.8 as Equation 4.10.

$$(I - M)Z = E \tag{4.10}$$

Finally, by rearranging terms, we arrive at the multiplier formula in Equation 4.11.

$$Z = (I - M)^{-1}E \tag{4.11}$$

This formula tells us that, when exogenous demand E increases, then after taking all rounds of direct and indirect linkage effects into account, you will end up with a final increase in total demand equal to Z (that is, some multiple of the initial or direct shock). The information on linkage effects from the SAM is incorporated into the multiplier model through the coefficient matrix M. With this formula we can now calculate the size of multiplier effects far more quickly than we did in the previous task.

Task 4: Constructing an Unconstrained Multiplier Model

In Task 4, you will construct an unconstrained SAM multiplier model using matrix algebra. You will use a three-sector version of the Ghana SAM. The task is contained in the file "Task 4 Worksheet.xls." You will need to translate the mathematical equations presented above into Excel. All hints are included in blue on the worksheet. You also need to answer the questions in red at the bottom of the worksheet. Once you have completed the task, you can check your answers by looking at the "Task 4" worksheet in the file "Task 4 Solution.xls."

To complete this task, you will need to be familiar with using matrix algebra in Excel. There is a detailed step-by-step hint provided in the Excel worksheet. You will also need to know how to use the MINVERSE and MMULT Excel functions. MINVERSE inverts a matrix, and MMULT multiplies two matrices together. You are alerted in the worksheet when these functions will be needed. Additional help on these and other matrix calculations can be found using the Excel help menu.

Discussion of Task 4

The final table in Part 3 of the solution worksheet shows the total multipliers. The agricultural output multiplier is initially equal to 2.42. This means that a direct increase in exogenous agricultural demand by 1 million cedi leads to a total increase in output by 2.42 million cedi once all linkages and round-by-round effects are taken into account. By contrast, the industrial output multiplier is only 1.25, even though the initial increase in exogenous demand is also 1 million cedi. These differences across sectors highlight the importance of taking multiplier effects into account when determining the overall impact of exogenous demand shocks. Notice also that the income multipliers for all sectors are lower than the output multiplier, due to various leakages from the circular flow of income (for instance, import and tax leakages).

There is another worksheet in the solution file called "Task 4 (advanced)." On this sheet we extend the multiplier model by allowing you to decide which components of demand should be treated as endogenous and which should be exogenous. You make a component exogenous by entering 1 into the table in Part 4 of the worksheet (shaded in gray). Conversely, you make a demand component endogenous by setting the cell entry to zero. If we set government demand to be endogenous, we can compare the size of the multipliers from the multiplier model where all three demand components are exogenous. We see now that the multipliers are larger because increased tax revenues raise government consumption demand, which then stimulates additional production in the service sector (because the government only consumes services). Ultimately, the more components of demand you set as endogenous, the larger the multiplier effects will be.

NOTE

8. Typical institutions in a SAM include households, government, and rest of the world. Government and rest of the world are typically aggregate entities in SAMs. Households, on the other hand, are often disaggregated into different groups in order to capture distributional impacts (by location, region, income percentiles, etc).

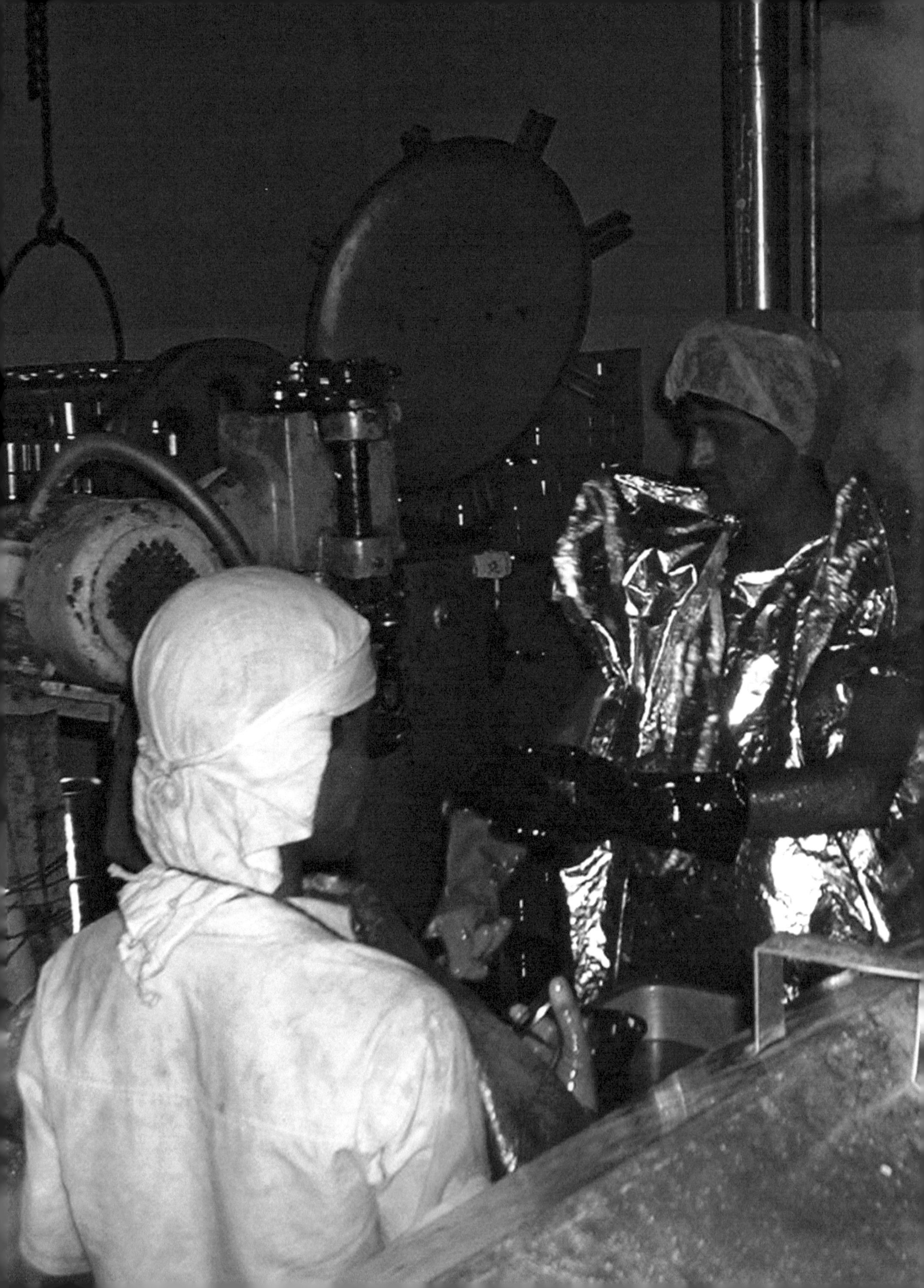

Exercise 5: Constrained SAM Multiplier Analysis

Deriving the Constrained Multiplier Formula

In the unconstrained multiplier model, we made a number of assumptions. One limitation of these was the assumption that supply is able to respond to changes in demand or that supply capacity is infinite given existing resources. In reality, this is rarely the case, especially because some sectors used specialized resources. For example, increasing demand for gold exports from Ghana may not lead to increased mining production if additional gold deposits do not exist or if the necessary investments in mining equipment have not been made. Moreover, increasing production in some sectors may lead to falling production in others if some resources are scarce. For example, increasing production of export crops, such as sugarcane, may require a reallocation of land away from foodcrop production, which may not be possible. In these cases, the supply response may not be unconstrained, and the suitability of the simple multiplier model from Exercise 4 becomes questionable. By ignoring supply constraints, unconstrained SAM-multiplier models typically overstate the impacts of linkage effects. Haggblade, Hammer, and Hazell (1991) find that these models overestimate agricultural growth multipliers by a factor of between two and ten.

In this final exercise, we drop the assumption that sectors' supply responses are unconstrained by fixing the level of output in certain sectors. This requires some adjustments to our multiplier formula to derive a constrained multiplier model. Although this class of models is often referred to as a "semi-input-output model," we will still derive a SAM-based multiplier formula.

Unconstrained multiplier formula

We now consider how the multiplier formula changes if some producing sectors are unable to respond to changes in demand (that is, supply is entirely constrained). Equation 4.7 from Exercise 4 expressed total demand as the sum of its parts.

$$\begin{aligned}(1-a_{11}b_1-c_1v_1b_1)Z_1+(-a_{12}b_2-c_1v_2b_2)Z_2&=E_1\\(-a_{21}b_1-c_2v_1b_1)Z_1+(1-a_{22}b_2-c_2v_2b_2)Z_2&=E_2\end{aligned}\tag{4.7}$$

We now distinguish between sectors that can change their production level (Z_1) and those sectors with supply constraints (Z_2). For fixed sectors, imports now substitute for fixed domestic supply. We therefore redefine all the components of demand that were previously treated as exogenous (E_2) to now be endogenous. In other words, net exports will now be able to change if domestic production cannot. As with the unconstrained multiplier formula, we group all exogenous components onto the right-hand side. This now includes the terms containing the constrained sectors (Z_2) and excludes the previously defined exogenous terms (E_2). This rearrangement is shown in Equations 5.1.

$$\begin{aligned}(1-a_{11}b_1-c_1v_1b_1)Z_1&=E_1+(a_{12}b_2+c_1v_2b_2)Z_2\\(-a_{21}b_1-c_2v_1b_1)Z_1-E_2&=-(1-a_{22}b_2-c_2v_2b_2)Z_2\end{aligned}\tag{5.1}$$

Equation 5.2 expresses Equation 5.1 in matrix format.

$$\begin{pmatrix}1-a_{11}b_1-c_1v_1b_1 & 0\\ -a_{21}b_1-c_2v_1b_1 & -1\end{pmatrix}\begin{pmatrix}Z_1\\E_2\end{pmatrix}=\begin{pmatrix}1 & a_{12}b_2+c_1v_2b_2\\ 0 & -1+a_{22}b_2+c_2v_2b_2\end{pmatrix}\begin{pmatrix}E_1\\Z_2\end{pmatrix}\tag{5.2}$$

The first term on the left-hand side of Equation 5.2 is the identity matrix (I) minus an adjusted coefficient matrix (M*).

$$\begin{pmatrix}1-a_{11}b_1-c_1v_1b_1 & 0\\ -a_{21}b_1-c_2v_1b_1 & -1\end{pmatrix}=I-M^*\tag{5.3}$$

The first term on the right-hand side of Equation 5.2 is a new term that we will abbreviate using B.

$$\begin{pmatrix} 1 & a_{12}b_2 + c_1v_2b_2 \\ 0 & -1 + a_{22}b_2 + c_2v_2b_2 \end{pmatrix} = B \tag{5.4}$$

Substituting the above two equations into Equation 5.2 gives Equation 5.5.

$$(I - M^*)\begin{pmatrix} Z_1 \\ E_2 \end{pmatrix} = B\begin{pmatrix} E_1 \\ Z_2 \end{pmatrix} \tag{5.5}$$

Finally, by rearranging terms, we arrive at the constrained multiplier formula in Equation 5.6.

$$\begin{pmatrix} Z_1 \\ E_2 \end{pmatrix} = (I - M^*)^{-1}B\begin{pmatrix} E_1 \\ Z_2 \end{pmatrix} \tag{5.6}$$

This equation tells us that an exogenous increase in demand for the unconstrained sectors (E_1) leads to a final increase in total demand for these sectors (Z_1), including all of the forward and backward linkages. However, for the sectors with constrained supply (Z_2), it is net exports (E_2) that decline; imports increase to replace the shortfall in domestic production. Because exports are now included inside exogenous demand, the equations solve for the impact of a change in demand (Z_2) on net exports (E_2), rather than the other way around.

TASK 5: INTERPRETING RESULTS FROM A CONSTRAINED MULTIPLIER MODEL

In Task 5, you will examine economywide growth linkages using a seven-sector SAM of Ghana (the detailed SAM used in Exercise 2). The semi-input-output model that you will need to answer this task's questions has already been programmed for you in Excel. You can find this constrained multiplier model in the file "Task 5 Worksheet.xls."

Ghana, like many developing countries, has a national development plan that places considerable emphasis on accelerating economic growth while also reducing poverty. Agriculture-led growth accompanied by growth in the food-processing industries is at the core of Ghana's development strategy. However, evidence from other countries shows that growth in other sectors will be needed to sustain economic growth. Consequently, Ghana's strategy also identifies mining, textiles, and tourism as potential sources of growth. However, there is little quantitative evidence identifying which sectors can most effectively contribute to economywide growth and income generation. In Task 5, you will use the constrained multiplier model to assess three alternative expansion scenarios for the Ghanaian economy:

1. *Increase in agricultural exports:* Simulate an increase in agricultural exports by 1 million cedi (one unit in the SAM). You should assume that the supply of government services is constrained (fixed) and that government consumption, net exports, and investment are all exogenous components of demand. Compare and discuss Ghana's strategy of expanding agriculture in light of your estimated output multipliers; GDP multipliers for labor and capital; and income multipliers for rural and urban households.

2. *Increase in manufacturing exports (Agriculture elastic):* Simulate an increase in manufacturing exports by 1 million cedi (one unit in the model). You should again assume that the supply of government services is constrained and that government consumption, net exports, and investment are all exogenous components of demand. Compare your estimated manufacturing multipliers to those of agriculture from question 1 above. Why is an expansion of agricultural exports more effective at stimulating economywide growth than manufacturing exports?

3. *Increase in manufacturing exports with constrained agricultural production (Agriculture inelastic):* Simulate an increase in manufacturing exports by 1 million cedi (one unit in the model). You should assume that the supply of both agriculture and government services is constrained and that government consumption, net exports, and investment are all exogenous components of demand. Compare your findings to the results from question 1 above. How have the various multipliers been affected by constraining the agricultural sector? What would this mean for a development strategy in Ghana focused exclusively on manufacturing-led growth?

To implement the three scenarios and answer the questions, you should (1) select which sectors are supply-constrained (that is, outside of the multiplier process); and then (2) select which components of demand are exogenous. Three general rules apply when running scenarios using the constrained multiplier model:

1. At least one of the three components of demand (government consumption, net exports, or investment) has to be exogenous.

2. It is reasonable to assume that the production of government services is always constrained and/or that government consumption is an exogenous component of demand.

3. The more components of demand that are endogenous, the larger the multiplier effect (see the discussion at the end of Task 4).

Once you have completed the task, you can check your answers comparing your results to those in Table 5 below.

Discussion of Task 5

Table 5 reports the results of the seven-sector constrained Ghana model. Model results for the three scenarios are reported in each column. These results are interpreted as follows: a one-unit increase in exogenous export demand leads to an increase in output, GDP, and household incomes as indicated in the respective column cell. The output multipliers add up all linkage effects to estimate the overall increase in gross output for each sector. The GDP multipliers combine all labor and capital earnings generated by the additional production in all sectors. Finally, the income multipliers measure the additional incomes generated by rural and urban households in each scenario.

In the three simulations, we compare an increase in agricultural exports and manufacturing exports. An increase in agricultural exports leads to a higher economywide GDP compared to manufacturing. While a 1 million-cedi increase in agricultural exports increases GDP by 1.19 million cedi, the same increase in manufacturing exports increases GDP by 0.32 million cedi. Moreover, if agricultural supply is constrained, then the impact of manufacturing exports on GDP is even smaller (0.18 million cedi).

A closer look at the results explains these differences in multiplier effects (see Table 5). Agriculture has stronger

Table 5. Multipliers under the three export expansion scenarios

		Scenario 1	Scenario 2	Scenario 3	
		Increased agricultural exports	Increased manufacturing exports		
			Agriculture elastic	Agriculture inelastic	
Activity - agriculture	aagr	1.34	0.16	0.00	Output
Activity - mining	amin	0.00	0.00	0.00	multipliers
Activity - manufacturing	aman	0.24	0.43	0.40	
Activity - electricity & water	aelw	0.07	0.05	0.04	
Activity - construction	acon	0.37	0.12	0.08	
Activity - public services	apubs	0.01	0.00	0.00	
Activity - private services	aprvs	0.16	0.04	0.02	
Commodity - agriculture	cagr	1.48	0.18	–0.12	Demand
Commodity - mining	cmin	0.00	0.00	0.00	multipliers
Commodity - manufacturing	cman	0.75	1.31	1.22	
Commodity - electricity & water	celw	0.07	0.05	0.04	
Commodity - construction	ccon	0.40	0.13	0.08	
Commodity - public services	cpubs	0.01	0.00	0.00	
Commodity - private services	cprvs	0.18	0.05	0.03	
Factor - labor	lab	1.03	0.24	0.12	GDP
Factor - capital	cap	0.16	0.08	0.06	multipliers
Households - rural	hrur	0.60	0.16	0.08	Income
Households - urban	hurb	0.59	0.16	0.09	multipliers
Government	gov	0.23	0.21	0.18	
Savings/investment	s-i	0.24	0.06	0.04	
Rest of world	row	0.54	0.73	0.66	Imports
Total multipliers	Output	2.19	0.80	0.54	
	GDP	1.19	0.32	0.18	

linkages to almost all sectors. The decomposition of agriculture's multiplier effect indicates that raising agricultural export demand by 1 million cedi causes agricultural output to increase by 1.34 million cedi, manufacturing to increase by 0.24 million cedi, construction by 0.37 million cedi, and private services by 0.16 million cedi. The total output multiplier effect is 2.19, meaning that the 1 million-cedi expansion of agricultural exports leads to a more than twofold overall increase in national output once all linkages are accounted for.

The change in total demand following increased agricultural exports is larger than the change in output, indicating that not all additional demand generated by agriculture's export expansion is supplied by domestic producers. This is particularly true for manufactured goods, where demand increases by 0.75 million cedi, but domestic output only grows by 0.24 million cedi. This reflects the high import intensity of manufacturing in Ghana. Urban households benefit almost as much as rural households from the increase in agricultural export demand. Rural household incomes increase by 0.60 million cedi, as compared to 0.59 million cedi for urban households.

Increasing manufacturing export demand has weaker domestic multiplier effects because much of the additional demand is met by imports. Assuming unconstrained or supply-elastic agriculture (Scenario 2), a 1 million-cedi increase in manufacturing export demand increases domestic agricultural output by 0.16 million cedi. This in turn induces additional production in other sectors, particularly in construction. This can be seen from the difference in output multipliers between Scenario 2, where agriculture's supply is unconstrained, and Scenario 3, where agriculture's supply is constrained. The GDP multiplier for manufacturing is higher for labor than for capital, reflecting the higher labor-intensity of manufacturing production. There is little difference in income effects across rural and urban households. The two household groups' incomes rise by 0.16 million cedi when agriculture is unconstrained and by 0.08 and 0.09 million cedi, respectively, when agriculture is constrained.

Comparing the two manufacturing export scenarios reveals the importance of agriculture as a means of expanding national GDP and raising household incomes. This is because agriculture has strong linkages to the rest of the economy. More specifically, agriculture's production and consumption linkages are directed toward sectors and institutions that use large shares of domestically produced goods and services. By contrast, manufacturing has large leakages resulting from the sector's high import intensity. Thus, most additional intermediate demand for manufacturing is supplied by domestic farmers, whose incomes rise accordingly. The same applies to private services and the electricity and water sectors, all of which are traded less than most other sectors.

Expanding agricultural export demand benefits household incomes more than manufacturing export growth. Moreover, because rural households spend a larger share of their income on agricultural goods and less on import-intensive manufactures, the expansion of agriculture leads to stronger consumption linkages and to fewer leakages. By contrast, expanding manufacturing exports leads to greater demand for imported manufactured intermediates. Together these weaker production and consumption linkages reduce the size of manufacturing's multiplier effects. Ultimately, our multiplier analysis confirms the need to target agriculture-led growth if Ghana wants to substantially raise economywide growth and improve household incomes.

References

Bautista, R. M. 2001. Agriculture-based development: A SAM perspective on Central Vietnam. *Journal of Development Economics* 39 (1): 112–132.

Breisinger, C., J. Thurlow, and M. Duncan. 2007. *A 2005 social accounting matrix (SAM) for Ghana*. Accra, Ghana, and Washington, D.C.: Ghana Statistical Services and International Food Policy Research Institute.

Diao, X., B. Fekadu, S. Haggblade, A. S. Taffesse, K. Wamisho, and B. Yu. 2007. *Agricultural growth linkages in Ethiopia: Estimates using fixed and flexible price models*. IFPRI Discussion Paper 695. Washington, D.C.: International Food Policy Research Institute.

Haggblade, S., and P. Hazell. 1989. Agricultural technology and farm-non-farm growth linkages. *Agricultural Economics* 3 (4): 345–364.

Haggblade, S., J. Hammer, and P. Hazell. 1991. Modeling agricultural growth multipliers. *American Journal of Agricultural Economics* 73 (2): 361–74.

Pyatt, G., and J. Round. 1985. *Social accounting matrices: A basis for planning*. Washington, D.C.: World Bank.

Reinert, K.A., and D.W. Roland-Holst. 1997. Social accounting matrices. In *Applied methods for trade policy analysis: A handbook*, ed. J.F. Francois and K.A. Reinert. New York: Cambridge University Press.

Robinson, S., A. Cattaneo, and M. El-Said. 2001. Updating and estimating a social accounting matrix using cross entropy methods. *Economic Systems Research* 13 (1): 47–64.

UNCTAD (United Nations Conference on Trade and Development). 2006. COMTRADE database. http://unstats.un.org/unsd/comtrade. Accessed December 7, 2009.

Appendix 1: Equation System for Unconstrained SAM Multiplier

We replace actual numbers in the SAM with the following symbols

	Activities A1	A2	Commodities C1	C2	Factors F	Households H	Exogenous demand E	Total
A1			X_1					X_1
A2				X_2				X_2
C1	Z_{11}	Z_{12}				C_1	E_1	Z_1
C2	Z_{21}	Z_{22}				C_2	E_2	Z_2
F	V_1	V_2						V
H					$V_1 + V_2$			Y
E			L_1	L_2		S		E
Total	X_1	X_2	Z_1	Z_2	V	Y	E	

We divide columns by their total to derive the coefficients matrix (M-matrix). Note that the M-matrix excludes the exogenous components of demand.

	Activities A1	A2	Commodities C1	C2	Factors F	Households H	Exogenous demand E	Total
A1			$b_1=X_1/Z_1$					X_1
A2				$b_2=X_2/Z_2$				X_2
C1	$a_{11}=Z_{11}/X_1$	$a_{12}=Z_{12}/X_2$				$c_1=C_1/Y$	E_1	Z_1
C2	$a_{21}=Z_{21}/X_1$	$a_{22}=Z_{22}/X_2$				$c_2=C_2/Y$	E_2	Z_2
F	$v_1=V_1/X_1$	$v_2=V_2/X_2$						V
H					1			Y
E			$l_1=L_1/Z_1$	$l_2=L_2/Z_2$		$s=S/Y$		E
Total	1	1	1	1	1	1	E	

Values

- X Gross output of each activity (i.e., X_1 and X_2)
- Z Total demand for each commodity (i.e., Z_1 and Z_2)
- V Total factor income (equal to household income)
- Y Total household income (equal to total factor income)
- E Exogenous components of demand (i.e., government, investment, and exports)

Shares

- a Technical coefficients (i.e., input or intermediate shares in production)
- b Share of domestic output in total demand
- v Share of value-added or factor income in gross output
- l Share of the value of total demand from imports or commodity taxes
- c Household consumption expenditure shares
- s Household savings rate (i.e., savings as a share of household income)

So we can now derive equations representing the relationships in the SAM. We start with the simple demand equations.

$$Z_1 = a_{11}X_1 + a_{12}X_2 + c_1Y + E_1$$
$$Z_2 = a_{21}X_1 + a_{22}X_2 + c_2Y + E_2 \quad \text{(A1)}$$

Total demand = intermediate demand + household demand + exogenous demand

From the SAM, we know that domestic production X is only part of total demand Z.

$$X_1 = b_1Z_1 \quad \text{and} \quad X_2 = b_2Z_2$$

We know that household income Y depends on the share each factor earns in each sector.

$$Y = v_1X_1 + v_2X_2 \quad \text{or} \quad Y = v_1b_1Z_1 + v_2b_2Z_2$$

Now we replace Xs and Ys in Equation A1.

$$Z_1 = a_{11}b_1Z_1 + a_{12}b_2Z_2 + c_1(v_1b_1Z_1 + v_2b_2Z_2) + E_1$$
$$Z_2 = a_{21}b_1Z_1 + a_{22}b_2Z_2 + c_2(v_1b_1Z_1 + v_2b_2Z_2) + E_2$$

We move everything except for E onto the left-hand side.

$$Z_1 - a_{11}b_1Z_1 - c_1v_1b_1Z_1 - a_{12}b_2Z_2 - c_1v_2b_2Z_2 = E_1$$
$$-a_{21}b_1Z_1 - c_2v_1b_1Z_1 + Z_2 - a_{22}b_2Z_2 - c_2v_2b_2Z_2 = E_2$$

We group Zs together.

$$(1 - a_{11}b_1 - c_1v_1b_1)Z_1 + (-a_{12}b_2 - c_1v_2b_2)Z_2 = E_1$$
$$(-a_{21}b_1 - c_2v_1b_1)Z_1 + (1 - a_{22}b_2 - c_2v_2b_2)Z_2 = E_2 \quad \text{(A2)}$$

We express Equation A2 in matrix format.

$$\begin{pmatrix} 1 - a_{11}b_1 - c_1v_1b_1 & -a_{12}b_2 - c_1v_2b_2 \\ -a_{21}b_1 - c_2v_1b_1 & 1 - a_{22}b_2 - c_2v_2b_2 \end{pmatrix} \begin{pmatrix} Z_1 \\ Z_2 \end{pmatrix} = \begin{pmatrix} E_1 \\ E_2 \end{pmatrix} \quad \text{(A3)}$$

The first term in Equation A3 is the identity matrix (I) minus the coefficient matrix (M).

$$\begin{pmatrix} 1 - a_{11}b_1 - c_1v_1b_1 & -a_{12}b_2 - c_1v_2b_2 \\ -a_{21}b_1 - c_2v_1b_1 & 1 - a_{22}b_2 - c_2v_2b_2 \end{pmatrix} = I - M$$

If we rename the other two vectors Z and E then we can simplify Equation A3.

$$(I - M)Z = E \quad \text{(A4)}$$

Rearranging, we get the final multiplier equation.

$$Z = (I - M)^{-1}E \quad \text{(A5)}$$

Total demand = multiplier matrix × exogenous demand

This tells us that when exogenous demand [E] increases, then after you have taken all the direct and indirect multiplier effects into account [$(I-M)^{-1}$], you will end up with a final increase in total demand equal to Z.

Appendix 2: Equation System for Constrained SAM Multiplier

We now consider how the multiplier changes if some producing sectors are unable to respond to changes in demand or are supply constrained. For fixed sectors (Z_2), imports substitute for domestic supply, thus eliminating any growth linkages from this sector.

Equation A2 from Appendix 1 expressed total demand as the sum of its parts.

$$\begin{aligned}(1 - a_{11}b_1 - c_1v_1b_1)Z_1 + (-a_{12}b_2 - c_1v_2b_2)Z_2 = E_1 \\ (-a_{21}b_1 - c_2v_1b_1)Z_1 + (1 - a_{22}b_2 - c_2v_2b_2)Z_2 = E_2\end{aligned} \qquad \text{(A2)}$$

We group exogenous terms on the right-hand side (i.e., E_1 and Z_2).

$$\begin{aligned}(1 - a_{11}b_1 - c_1v_1b_1)Z_1 = E_1 + (a_{12}b_2 + c_1v_2b_2)Z_2 \\ (-a_{21}b_1 - c_2v_1b_1)Z_1 - E_2 = -(1 - a_{22}b_2 - c_2v_2b_2)Z_2\end{aligned} \qquad \text{(A6)}$$

We express Equation A6 in matrix format.

$$\begin{pmatrix}1 - a_{11}b_1 - c_1v_1b_1 & 0 \\ -a_{21}b_1 - c_2v_1b_1 & -1\end{pmatrix}\begin{pmatrix}Z_1 \\ E_2\end{pmatrix} = \begin{pmatrix}1 & a_{12}b_2 + c_1v_2b_2 \\ 0 & -1 + a_{22}b_2 + c_2v_2b_2\end{pmatrix}\begin{pmatrix}E_1 \\ Z_2\end{pmatrix} \qquad \text{(A7)}$$

The first term in Equation A7 is the identity matrix (I) minus an *adjusted* M-matrix.

$$\begin{pmatrix}1 - a_{11}b_1 - c_1v_1b_1 & 0 \\ -a_{21}b_1 - c_2v_1b_1 & -1\end{pmatrix} = I - M^* \qquad \text{(A7.1)}$$

The first term on the right-hand side of A7.1 is a new term called B.

$$\begin{pmatrix}1 & a_{12}b_2 + c_1v_2b_2 \\ 0 & -1 + a_{22}b_2 + c_2v_2b_2\end{pmatrix} = B \qquad \text{(A7.2)}$$

Simplifying Equation A7.2, we now get the equation below.

$$(I - M^*)\begin{pmatrix}Z_1 \\ E_2\end{pmatrix} = B\begin{pmatrix}E_1 \\ Z_2\end{pmatrix} \qquad \text{(A7.3)}$$

Rearranging, we get the new constrained multiplier equation.

$$\begin{pmatrix}Z_1 \\ E_2\end{pmatrix} = (I - M^*)^{-1}B\begin{pmatrix}E_1 \\ Z_2\end{pmatrix} \qquad \text{(A8)}$$

This equation tells us that an exogenous increase in demand for the unconstrained sectors [E_1] leads to a final increase in total demand for these sectors [Z_1] including all of the forward and backward linkages [$(I-M^*)^{-1}$]. However, for the sectors with constrained supply, it is net exports that decline (that is, imports increase). Because exports are included inside exogenous demand [E_2], the equations solve for the impact of a change in demand [Z_2] on exports [E_2], rather than the other way around.

Photos

Page viii © 2008 Klaus von Grebmer/IFPRI
Page 6 © 2009 Jeremy Horner/Panos Pictures
Page 12 © 2005 Ashok Gulati/IFPRI
Page 16 © 2005 Richard Lord
Page 22 © 2005 Ashok Gulati/IFPRI

Made in the USA
Monee, IL
05 November 2026

67382736R00026